THIS BOOK BELONG

Self-Awareness Detective

The OFFICIAL Self-Awareness
Companion Journal for the
Kendry Uto, Detective Series

· TOP SECRET ·

For your own investigation
of self-awareness and
self-engagement as a highly
intelligent child.

WRITTEN & DESIGNED BY JULIA QUILLEN
ILLUSTRATED BY MARIA HECHER

For permission requests, write to the publisher, addressed "Attention: Permissions Coordinator," at the address below.
First Printing, August 2022

Paperback ISBN 978-1-959003-01-4

Cultivate Grace
bringing grace to life.

Cultivate Grace, LLC
464 Turner Avenue
Drexel Hill, PA 19026
www.CultivateGrace.org

We thank Ken Sande, the Founder and President of Relational Wisdom ® 360 and author of The Peacemaker, for permission to use Relational Wisdom resources in this book. For more information on Relational Wisdom® 360, please visit www.rw360.org.

References to Relational Wisdom principles and acronyms
© 2022 by Kenneth Sande and used by permission.

For Mike and our seven highly intelligent kids who fill my life and inspire so many lovely emotions.

Table of Contents

Using this Journal

Have you ever read a choose-your-own-adventure story? One where at the end of a page YOU decide what the character will do? It's usually something like: "If Mckenzie sneaks out to the treehouse, turn to page 7. If Mckenzie goes down to the river, turn to page 11." Then at the end of page 7 or 11—depending on which you chose—you are faced with another decision. (If you haven't ever read one of these stories, I highly recommend them!)

I like to think of this journal as *your own* Choose-Your-Own-Adventure story.

You might use it:

> ➤ To intentionally look for, or *reflect on*, something you did or felt so you can learn about yourself...and maybe recognize what you did well & want to repeat and/or what you did poorly and want to change (past focus)
> ➤ To think through, or *process*, a specific situation so you can choose how you want to move forward (present focus)
> ➤ To shape, or *prepare for*, a conversation you need to have or an action you need to take (future focus)

Whether you are learning from what has already happened, doing something right now, or preparing to speak or act, this journal can help you build skills to understand yourself and do what you *truly* want to do.

In the moment of big feelings, it's hard to figure out what we truly want. Our feelings encourage us to fight (attack), freeze (shut down), or flee (avoid).

It's important to react quickly when we *need* to act fast... like if you touch a hot cookie sheet, you need to snatch your hand back quickly so you don't get burned.

But sometimes our feelings encourage us to do something harmful instead of helpful. Like if you see a rattlesnake, our feelings encourage us to jump back (flee), when what we need to do is freeze, and then back away very slowly, so the snake is less threatened and doesn't strike.

So how do we get to the point where we can pause when we need to?

Picture a team of horses. Horses are good. Harnessed together and well trained they make a magnificent sight! Even better, they can pull a sleigh through thick snow, move a tree off the riverbank, or carry a load of Christmas trees down a mountain to a village. If they are spooked and don't obey their master—or if the master doesn't know how to guide them—they might fight each other, run wild, and take themselves and the whole load careening dangerously off the road.

Now let's imagine our emotions are the team of horses. Like horses, emotions are good. They are powerful. When trained and harnessed, they can work together to help us move heavy loads and get places quickly. However, untrained and unharnessed, all their power can get us into BIG trouble fast! That's why we need to train our emotions to take us where we want to go and learn how to guide them.

In the companion chapter book, *Kendry Uto, Detective: An Investigation of Self-Awareness for Highly Intelligent Children*, Kendry demonstrates how to reflect on something he did and felt in a specific situation so he could change the outcome. Focusing on the past helps him choose a new future. You can see **Kendry's Completed Chart** on pages 6-7.

As another example, in the **Sample Chart** on pages 8-9, Kendry uses the chart to decide how he wants to respond to his brother Viktor's hurtful question.

While he is experiencing his unrecognized emotions, Kendry wants to be rude, sarcastic, and punch Viktor.

Once he stops to recognize how he feels, Kendry figures out why he feels misunderstood, angry, and sad. He understands that what he *truly* wants, is to be able to ask a question and be treated with kindness.

Kendry *could* let his emotion-horses go wild, punch his brother, and speak rudely (and probably end up getting in trouble with his mom). *Or* Kendry could harness those emotion-horses and talk to Viktor about how his brother's words and tone hurt him.

Taking time to develop self-awareness empowers Kendry to ask for what he really wants.

So, let's think about Kendry's choices. Is Kendry more likely to get Viktor to talk to him with kindness and respect if he:

> A. Speaks sarcastically and punches him, or
> B. Says something like, "Viktor, when you use a rude tone of voice to ask if I heard what Mom said, it hurts my feelings. I feel judged, misunderstood, angry, and sad. I would rather you ask a curious question if you don't know why I'm asking something. That would feel better to me."

HINT: **B** is more likely to inspire Viktor to speak kindly. (But you knew that already, didn't you?)

To be honest, filling out the chart takes a bit of time—especially at first. As with any new skill, the more you do it, the better and faster you get. As you learn to complete the chart, you'll get better and faster at navigating big feelings and responding in ways that help you do what you want. With practice, you'll be able to reflect, process, and prepare in real time.

Even after you've mastered the skills of self-awareness (knowing what you feel & why) and self-engagement (seeing where actions could lead & making helpful choices) you may find the charts helpful from time to time when you encounter especially BIG things.

Whatever way makes sense for you to use this journal, I hope it equips you to master the skill of understanding and managing your emotions.

I'd love to hear about *your* adventure! Please email me at Julia@CultivateGrace.org to let me know how it's going for you.

How to Use the Charts

Color the doodles while you think. There's also room to add some of your own!

Describe the Circumstances
What actually happened? What are the FACTS about what someone or something did or said?

Here is where you explain it.

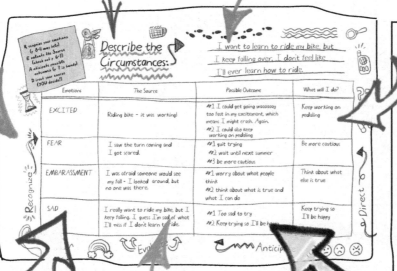

Describe the Circumstances:

I want to learn to ride my bike, but I keep falling over. I don't feel like I'll ever learn how to ride.

Emotions	The Source	Possible Outcome	What will I do?
EXCITED	Riding bike – it was working!	#1 I could get going waaaaay too fast in my excitement, which means I might crash. Again. #2 I could also keep working on pedaling	Keep working on pedaling
FEAR	I saw the turn coming and I got scared.	#1 quit trying #2 wait until next summer #3 be more cautious	Be more cautious
EMBARASSMENT	I was afraid someone would see my fall – I looked around, but no one was there.	#1 worry about what people think #2 think about what is true and what I can do	Think about what else is true
SAD	I really want to ride my bike, but I keep falling. I guess I'm sad of what I'll miss if I don't learn to ride.	#1 Too sad to try #2 Keep trying so I'll be happy	Keep trying so I'll be happy

Recognize

Evaluate

Anticipate

Direct

Recognize your Emotions
What is happening in your body?
What do you feel?

List your emotions by name here.

Evaluate the Source
Why do you think you feel _____ ?

Take notes on what is inspiring your feelings.

Anticipate the Outcome
What could happen if you do what you feel like doing?
What else could you do?
What might happen then?

Write that down here!

Direct your Course
Which of the outcomes you anticipated do you WANT to happen? What will you do to get there?

Don't forget to check back and make notes on the actual outcome after you did what you did.

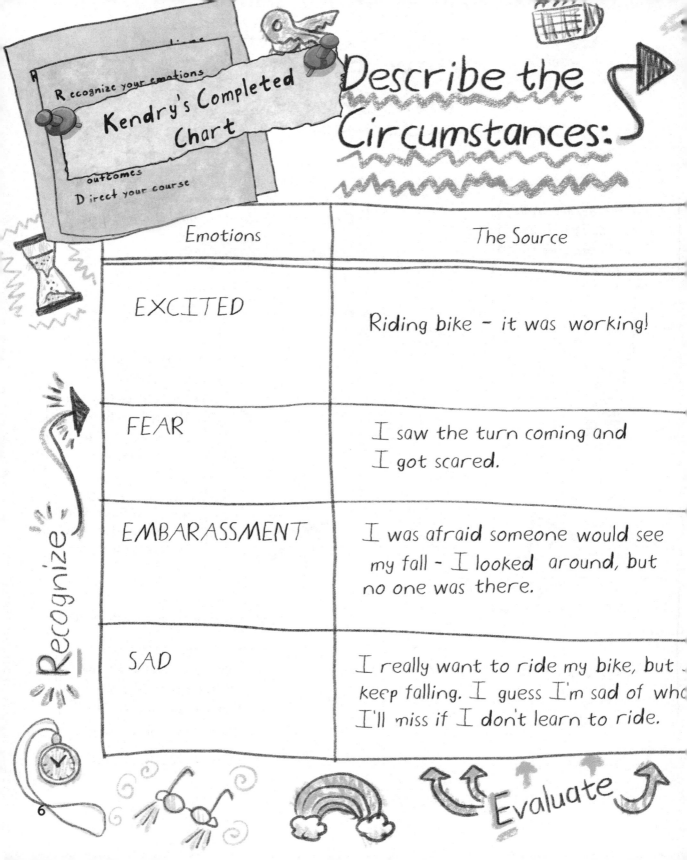

Kendry's Completed Chart

Recognize your emotions

outcomes
Direct your course

Describe the Circumstances:

Emotions	The Source
EXCITED	Riding bike – it was working!
FEAR	I saw the turn coming and I got scared.
EMBARASSMENT	I was afraid someone would see my fall – I looked around, but no one was there.
SAD	I really want to ride my bike, but I keep falling. I guess I'm sad of what I'll miss if I don't learn to ride.

Recognize

Evaluate

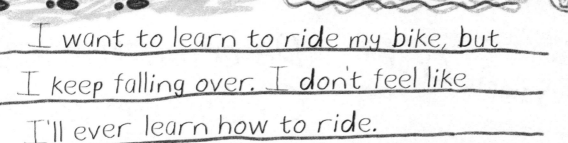

I want to learn to ride my bike, but I keep falling over. I don't feel like I'll ever learn how to ride.

Possible Outcome	What will I do?
#1 I could get going waaaaaay too fast in my excitement, which means I might crash. Again. #2 I could also keep working on pedaling	Keep working on pedaling
#1 quit trying #2 wait until next summer #3 be more cautious	Be more cautious
#1 worry about what people think #2 think about what is true and what I can do	Think about what else is true
#1 Too sad to try #2 Keep trying so I'll be happy	Keep trying so I'll be happy

Direct

Anticipate

7

Sample Chart

Describe the Circumstances:

Emotions	The Source
Misunderstood	I was trying to ask if we were going to eat lunch before we left for Oma's house, so I asked when we were going to leave after mom said we'd leave at lunchtime.
Angry	I am mad because I *DID* hear what Mom said. And Viktor said it in a rude way and I feel judged and like he thinks I am stupid.
Sad	I am sad because I wanted to know if we were eating lunch at home or not, but instead of answering me Viktor made fun of me.

Recognize

Evaluate

At breakfast, I asked a question and Viktor said, "Didn't you hear anything mom said?" in a really rude tone.

Possible Outcome	What will I do?
#1 - I could be rude back #2 - I could be sarcastic #3 - I could explain why I asked	I want to explain what I meant.
#1 - I could punch him in the face #2 - I could take a deep breath and think about how to talk to him about how his tone made me feel.	I want to talk to Viktor about how his tone sounded to me.
#1 - I could just go to my room #2 - I can remember it's ok to be hurt, and talk to Viktor about it.	I want to talk to Viktor about how it hurt my feelings and how I'd prefer that he talk to me.

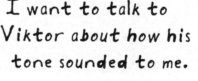
Direct

Anticipate

9

Detective Tools

Recognize your emotions

R Clue: What does your body feel? Do you have tight muscles? Butterflies in your belly? Tears? Hot/red face? Racing heartbeat? Huge smile? Wide eyes? (Check the emotions chart for ideas on the feelings that go with these clues from your body. List the emotion(s) in your chart.)

Evaluate the source

E Clue: What did you want that you are not getting? What are you afraid of losing/missing? How understood do you feel? What are you concerned others might be thinking? What words or actions came before you started feeling this? What feels unfair? What feels impossible? What hurts? What is scary? (Make a note in the chart of what is behind/under/inspiring each of the emotions you noted in your chart.)

Anticipate Possible Outcomes

A Clue: What do you feel like doing as a result of your emotions? What might happen if you do what you feel like doing? What else? What outcome would you like to see happen? What are other things you could do besides what you feel like doing? What have you tried before? How did that work out for you? What is something you could do to get the outcome you're hoping for? What else? (Try to find at least 3-5 ideas for actions and outcomes.)

Direct Your Course
Decide What You Want to Do

D Clue: When you look at the possible outcomes - which do you want most? What is the best way to get to that outcome?
What will you do? (Make a note of this in your chart.* If you think of it later, come back and write down how it turned out. This can be a great resource for choosing differently in the future if something doesn't work - or as a great start for repeating things that worked well!)

Important Investigation Questions

- What has happened?
- How would you describe the challenge?
- Why is this important to you?
- When has something similar happened?
- What do you expect will happen next?
- How are you feeling about that possibility?
- Are you believing a possible outcome has already happened?
- How can you clarify what has truly happened already?
- What else is true?
- Who is involved?
- What part did you add to the conflict/problem?
- What did others add to the conflict/problem?
- What motives are you assuming about others?
- What have you done to explore their true intent?
- What do you FEEL like doing?
- What do YOU want to happen?
- What is keeping that from happening?
- What are others wanting to have happen?
- What might satisfy everyone?
- How do you want to respond?
- What might help overcome the challenge?
- What can you find that is good about this?
- What hope do you have that things can be different?
- What else could happen?
- What are you really longing for?

Emotions Rainbow

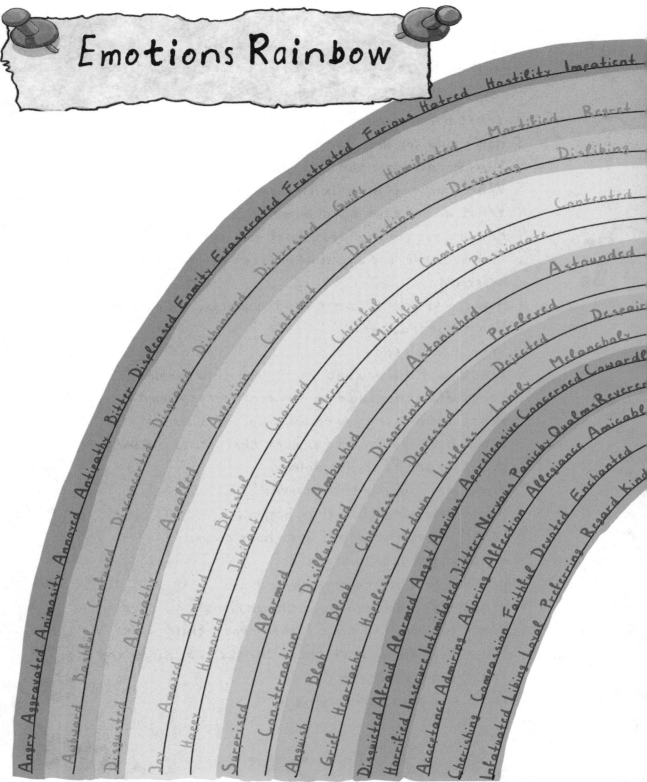

A radial emotion wheel with words written along concentric arcs, from the outermost ring inward:

Ring 1: Incensed · Indignant · Infuriated · Irked · Irritated · Mad · Miffed · Outraged · Resentment · Riled · Ticked-off · Vengeful · Vexed · Wrathful

Ring 2: Remorseful · Self-conscious · Shame · Embarrassed · Shy · Timid · Uncomfortable · Uneasy · Unworthy · Worthless

Ring 3: Distaste · Loathing · Objection · Rejection · Repulsed · Revulsion · Scandalized · Scorn

Ring 4: Delight · Diverted · Elated · Refreshed · Satisfied · Excitement · Exultant · Glad · Grateful · Gratified · Wonder

Ring 5: Pleased · Bewildered · Retreshed · Caotured · Thankful · Confused · Hander

Ring 6: Bemused · Shocked · Distressed · Stunned · Startled · Thrilled · Traced

Ring 7: Puzzled · Sad · Mournful · Doleful · Forlorn · Gloomy

Ring 8: Disappointed · Moody · Self-pity · Sorrowful · Unhappy

Ring 9: Miserable · Dispirited · Faint-hearted · Foreboding · Frightened · Worried

Ring 10: Dismayed · Fear · Doubt · Dread · Trepidation · Uneasy · Misgivings

Ring 11: Scared · Suspicious · Terrified · Tremble · Attraction · Captivated · Friendly

Ring 12: Love · Curious · Appreciation · Fidelity · Fondness · Glorifying

Ring 13: Esteeming · Amorous · Treasuring · Worshipful

Ring 14: Ardor · Respect · Zeal

Emotions Chart

Angry	Embarrassed	Disgusted	Joy
Aggravated	Awkward	Antipathy	Amazed
Animosity	Bashful	Appalled	Amused
Annoyed	Confused	Aversion	Blissful
Antipathy	Disconcerted	Contempt	Charmed
Bitter	Disgraced	Detesting	Cheerful
Displeased	Dishonored	Despising	Comforted
Enmity	Distressed	Disliking	Contented
Exasperated	Guilt	Distaste	Delight
Frustrated	Humiliated	Loathing	Diverted
Furious	Mortified	Objection	Elated
Hatred	Regret	Rejection	Excitement
Hostility	Remorseful	Repulsed	Exultant
Impatient	Self-conscious	Revulsion	Glad
Incensed	Shame	Scandalized	Grateful
Indignant	Shy	Scorn	Gratified
Infuriated	Timid		Happy
Irked	Uncomfortable		Humored
Irritated	Uneasy		Jubilant
Mad	Unworthy		Lively
Miffed	Worthless		Merry
Outraged			Mirthful
Resentment			Passionate
Riled			Pleased
Ticked-off			Refreshed
Vengeful			Satisfied
Vexed			Thankful
Wrathful			Thrilled
			Wonder

Surprised	Sad	Fear	Love
Alarmed	Anguish	Afraid	Acceptance
Ambushed	Blah	Alarmed	Admiring
Astonished	Bleak	Angst	Adoring
Astounded	Cheerless	Anxious	Affection
Bemused	Depressed	Apprehensive	Allegiance
Bewildered	Dejected	Concerned	Amicable
Captured	Despair	Cowardly	Amorous
Caught	Disappointed	Dismayed	Appreciation
Confused	Dispirited	Disquieted	Ardor
Consternation	Distressed	Doubt	Attraction
Disillusioned	Doleful	Dread	Captivated
Disoriented	Forlorn	Fainthearted	Cherishing
Perplexed	Gloomy	Foreboding	Compassion
Puzzled	Grief	Frightened	Curious
Shocked	Heartache	Horrified	Devoted
Stunned	Hopeless	Insecure	Enchanted
Startled	Let down	Intimidated	Esteeming
Trapped	Listless	Jittery	Faithful
	Lonely	Nervous	Fidelity
	Melancholy	Panicky	Fondness
	Miserable	Qualms	Friendly
	Moody	Reverence	Glorifying
	Mopey	Scared	Infatuated
	Mournful	Suspicious	Kind
	Self-pity	Terrified	Liking
	Sorrowful	Trembly	Loyal
	Unhappy	Trepidatious	Preferring
		Uneasy	Regard
		Worried	Respect
		Misgivings	Treasuring
			Worshipful
			Zeal

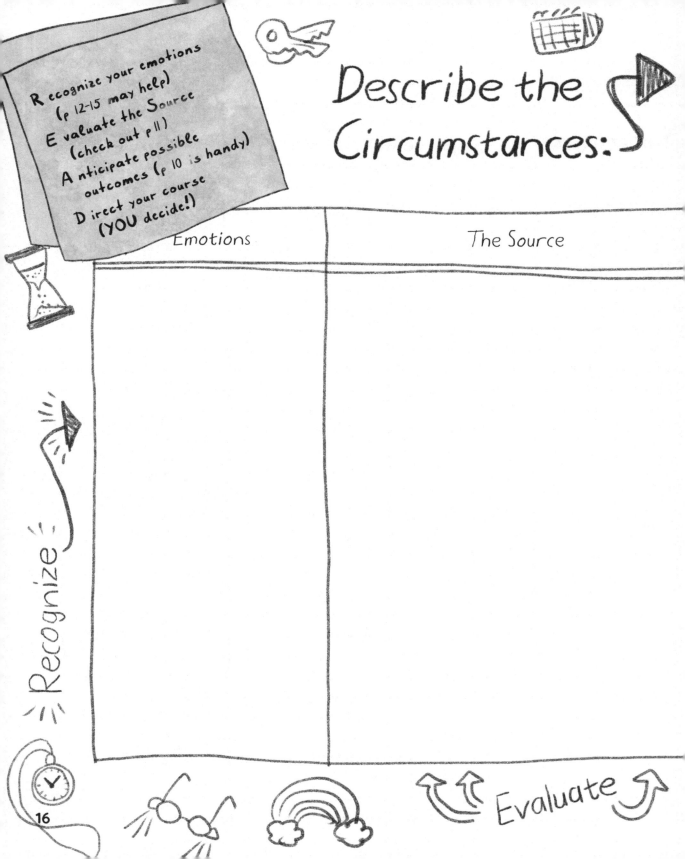

R ecognize your emotions
(p 12-15 may help)
E valuate the Source
(check out p 11)
A nticipate possible
outcomes (p 10 is handy)
D irect your course
(YOU decide!)

Describe the Circumstances:

Emotions	The Source

Recognize

Evaluate

Possible Outcome	What will I do?

Anticipate

Direct

17

R ecognize your emotions
(p 12-15 may help)
E valuate the Source
(check out p 11)
A nticipate possible
outcomes (p 10 is handy)
D irect your course
(YOU decide!)

Describe the Circumstances:

Emotions	The Source

Recognize

Evaluate

_____

_____

_____

_____

Possible Outcome	What will I do?

Anticipate

Direct

R ecognize your emotions
   (p 12-15 may help)
E valuate the Source
   (check out p 11)
A nticipate possible
   outcomes (p 10 is handy)
D irect your course
   (YOU decide!)

Describe the Circumstances:

Emotions	The Source

Recognize

Evaluate

Possible Outcome	What will I do?

Anticipate

Direct

R ecognize your emotions
   (p 12-15 may help)
E valuate the Source
   (check out p 11)
A nticipate possible
   outcomes (p 10 is handy)
D irect your course
   (YOU decide!)

Describe the Circumstances:

Emotions	The Source

Recognize

Evaluate

HELP

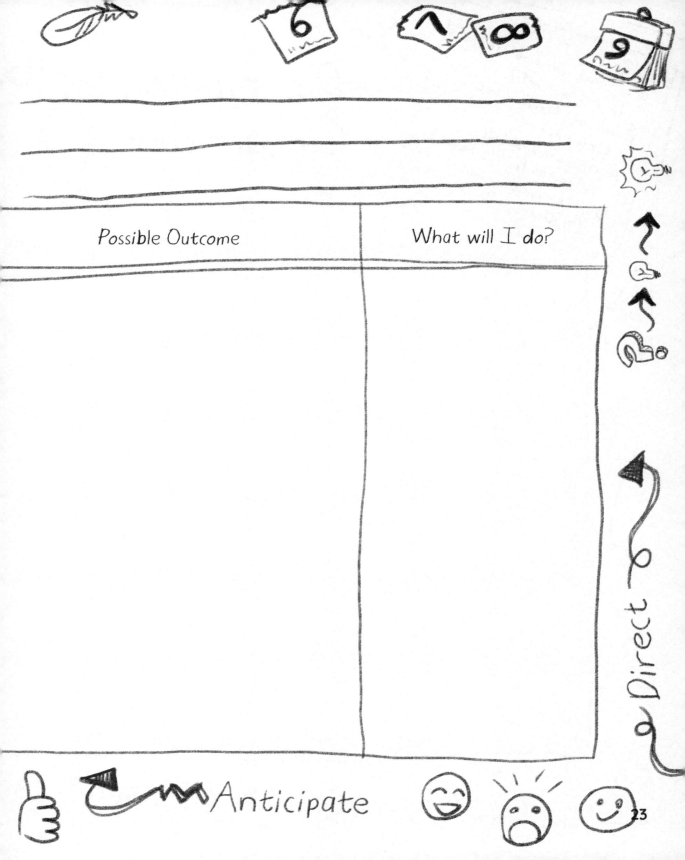

Possible Outcome	What will I do?

Anticipate

Direct

23

R ecognize your emotions
  (p 12-15 may help)
E valuate the Source
  (check out p 11)
A nticipate possible
  outcomes (p 10 is handy)
D irect your course
  (YOU decide!)

Describe the Circumstances:

Emotions	The Source

Recognize

Evaluate

Possible Outcome	What will I do?

Anticipate

Describe the Circumstances:

Emotions	The Source

Recognize

Evaluate

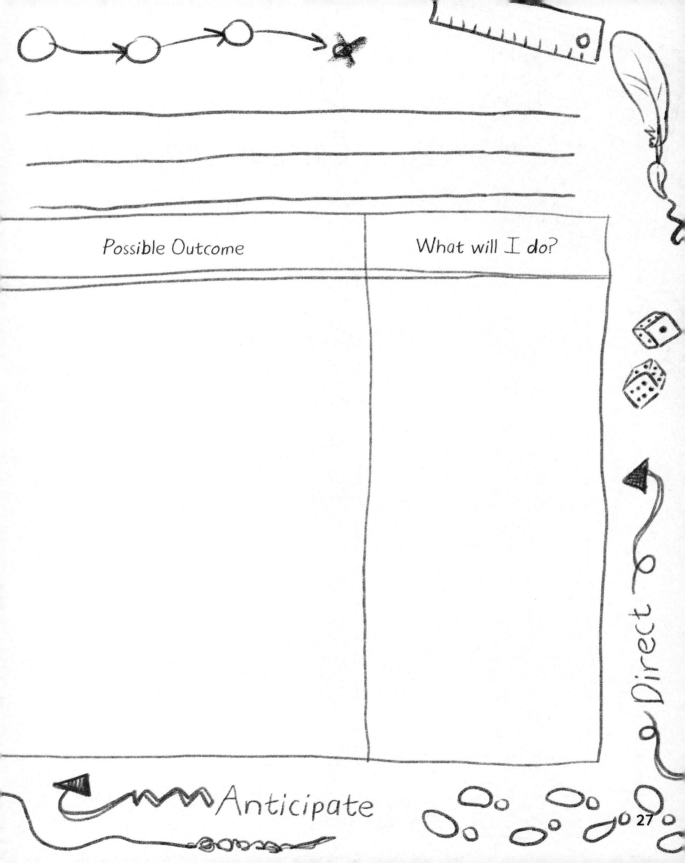

Possible Outcome	What will I do?

Anticipate

Direct

Describe the
Circumstances:

R ecognize your emotions
  (p 12-15 may help)
E valuate the Source
  (check out p 11)
A nticipate possible
  outcomes (p 10 is handy)
D irect your course
  (YOU decide!)

Emotions	The Source

Recognize

Evaluate

Possible Outcome	What will I do?

Direct

Anticipate

Recognize your emotions
(p 12-15 may help)
Evaluate the Source
(check out p 11)
Anticipate possible
outcomes (p 10 is handy)
Direct your course
(YOU decide!)

Describe the Circumstances:

Emotions	The Source

Recognize

HELP

Evaluate

30

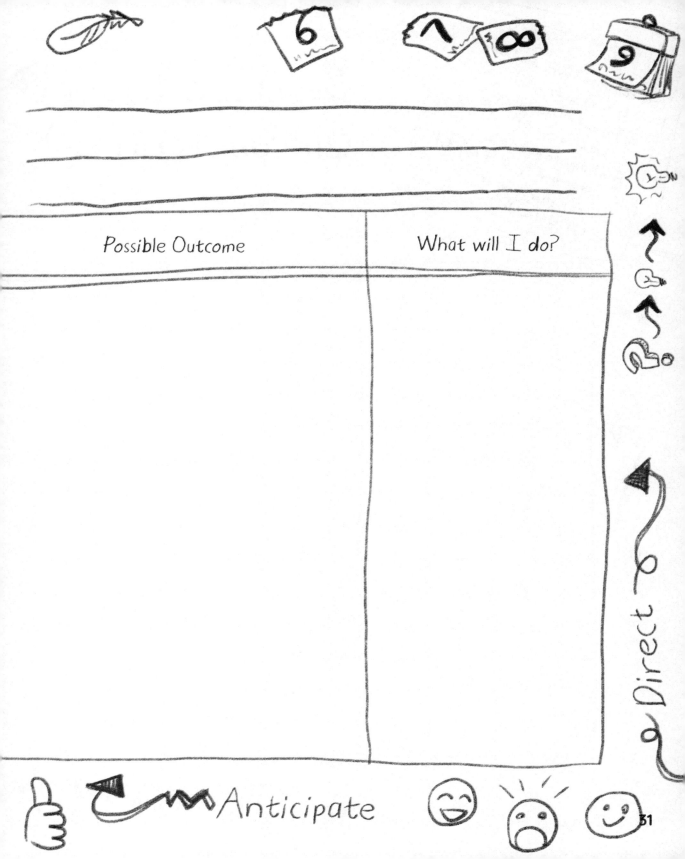

_____
_____
_____

Possible Outcome	What will I do?

Direct

Anticipate

R ecognize your emotions
(p 12-15 may help)
E valuate the Source
(check out p 11)
A nticipate possible
outcomes (p 10 is handy)
D irect your course
(YOU decide!)

Describe the Circumstances:

Emotions	The Source

Recognize

Evaluate

_____

_____

_____

Possible Outcome	What will I do?

Anticipate

Direct

Describe the Circumstances:

Emotions	The Source

Recognize

Evaluate

_____

_____

_____

Possible Outcome	What will I do?

Anticipate

Direct

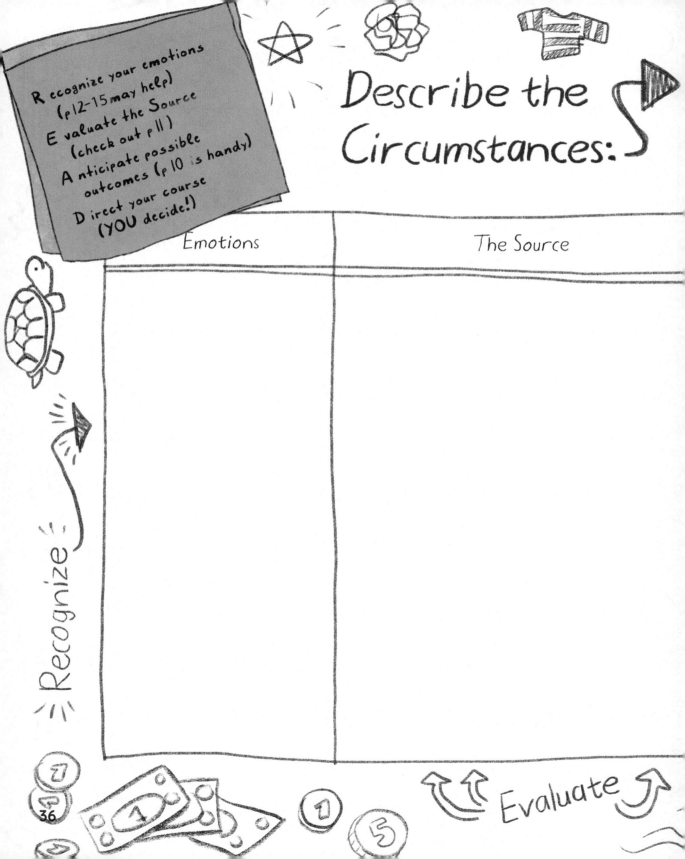

R ecognize your emotions
   (p 12-15 may help)
E valuate the Source
   (check out p 11)
A nticipate possible
   outcomes (p 10 is handy)
D irect your course
   (YOU decide!)

Describe the Circumstances:

Emotions	The Source

Recognize

Evaluate

Possible Outcome	What will I do?

Anticipate

Direct

R ecognize your emotions
    (p 12-15 may help)
E valuate the Source
    (check out p 11)
A nticipate possible
    outcomes (p 10 is handy)
D irect your course
    (YOU decide!)

Describe the Circumstances:

Emotions	The Source

Recognize

Evaluate

HELP

_____

_____

_____

Possible Outcome	What will I do?

Direct

Anticipate

R ecognize your emotions
   (p 12-15 may help)
E valuate the Source
   (check out p 11)
A nticipate possible
   outcomes (p 10 is handy)
D irect your course
   (YOU decide!)

Describe the Circumstances:

Emotions	The Source

Recognize

Evaluate

Possible Outcome	What will I do?

Direct

Anticipate

41

Recognize your emotions
(p 12-15 may help)
Evaluate the Source
(check out p 11)
Anticipate possible
outcomes (p 10 is handy)
Direct your course
(YOU decide!)

Describe the Circumstances:

Emotions	The Source

Recognize

Evaluate

Possible Outcome	What will I do?

Anticipate

Direct

43

R ecognize your emotions
   (p 12-15 may help)
E valuate the Source
   (check out p 11)
A nticipate possible
   outcomes (p 10 is handy)
D irect your course
   (YOU decide!)

Describe the Circumstances:

Emotions	The Source

Recognize

Evaluate

44

_____

_____

_____

Possible Outcome	What will I do?

Anticipate

Direct

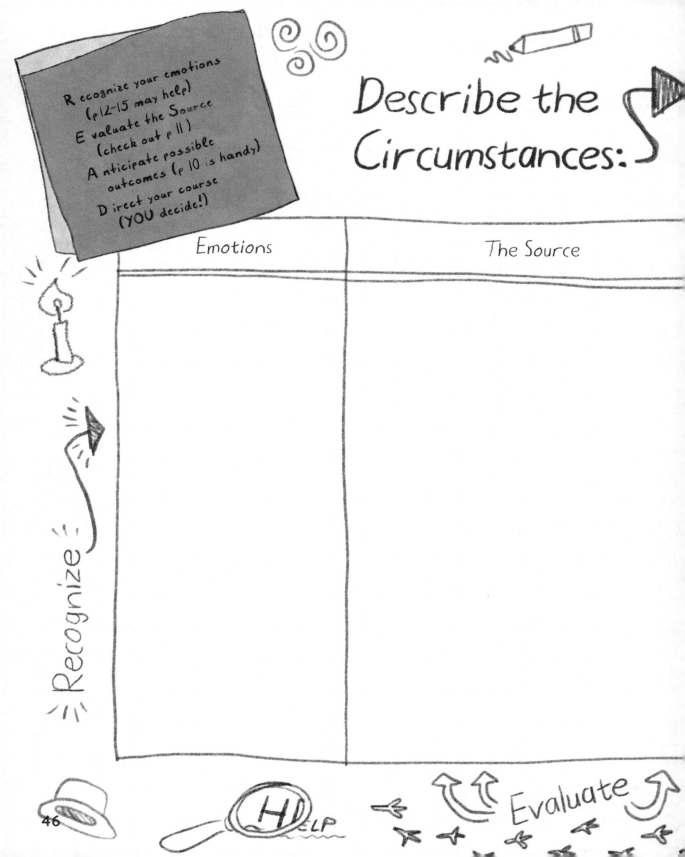

R ecognize your emotions
  (p 12-15 may help)
E valuate the Source
  (check out p 11)
A nticipate possible
  outcomes (p 10 is handy)
D irect your course
  (YOU decide!)

Describe the Circumstances:

Emotions	The Source

Recognize

HELP

Evaluate

46

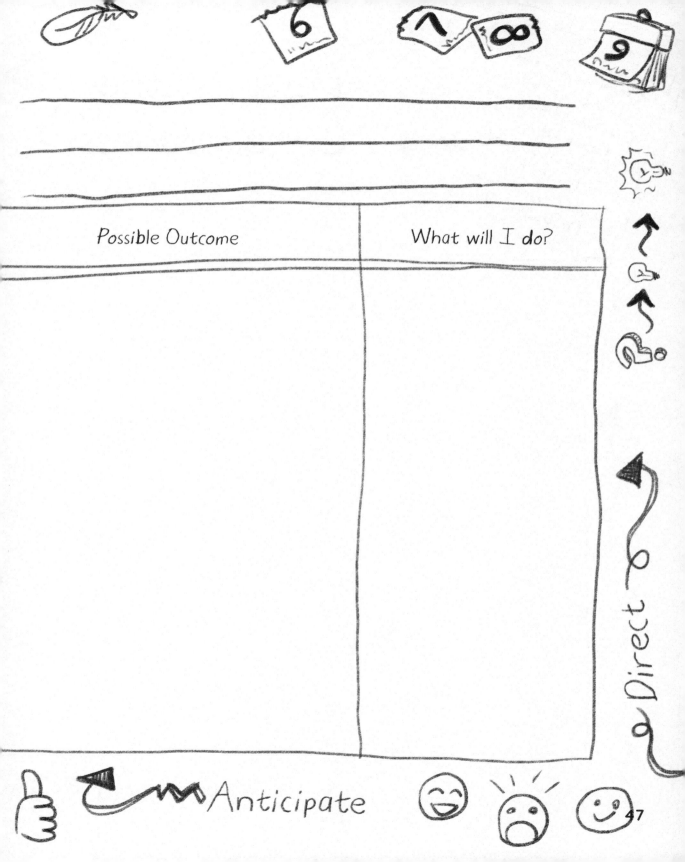

Possible Outcome	What will I do?

Direct

Anticipate

Recognize your emotions
(p 12-15 may help)
Evaluate the Source
(check out p 11)
Anticipate possible
outcomes (p 10 is handy)
Direct your course
(YOU decide!)

Describe the Circumstances:

Emotions	The Source

Recognize

Evaluate

Possible Outcome	What will I do?

Direct

Anticipate

49

R ecognize your emotions
(p 12-15 may help)
E valuate the Source
(check out p 11)
A nticipate possible
outcomes (p 10 is handy)
D irect your course
(YOU decide!)

Describe the Circumstances:

Emotions	The Source

Recognize

Evaluate

Possible Outcome	What will I do?

Anticipate

Direct

R ecognize your emotions
(p 12-15 may help)
E valuate the Source
(check out p 11)
A nticipate possible
outcomes (p 10 is handy)
D irect your course
(YOU decide!)

Describe the Circumstances:

Emotions	The Source

Recognize

Evaluate

52

_____

_____

_____

Possible Outcome	What will I do?

Anticipate

Direct

Recognize your emotions
(p12-15 may help)
Evaluate the Source
(check out p 11)
Anticipate possible
outcomes (p 10 is handy)
Direct your course
(YOU decide!)

Describe the Circumstances:

Emotions	The Source

Recognize

HELP

Evaluate

_____
_____
_____

Possible Outcome	What will I do?

Direct

Anticipate

Recognize your emotions
(p 12-15 may help)
Evaluate the Source
(check out p 11)
Anticipate possible
outcomes (p 10 is handy)
Direct your course
(YOU decide!)

Describe the Circumstances:

Emotions	The Source

Recognize

Evaluate

Possible Outcome	What will I do?

Anticipate

Direct

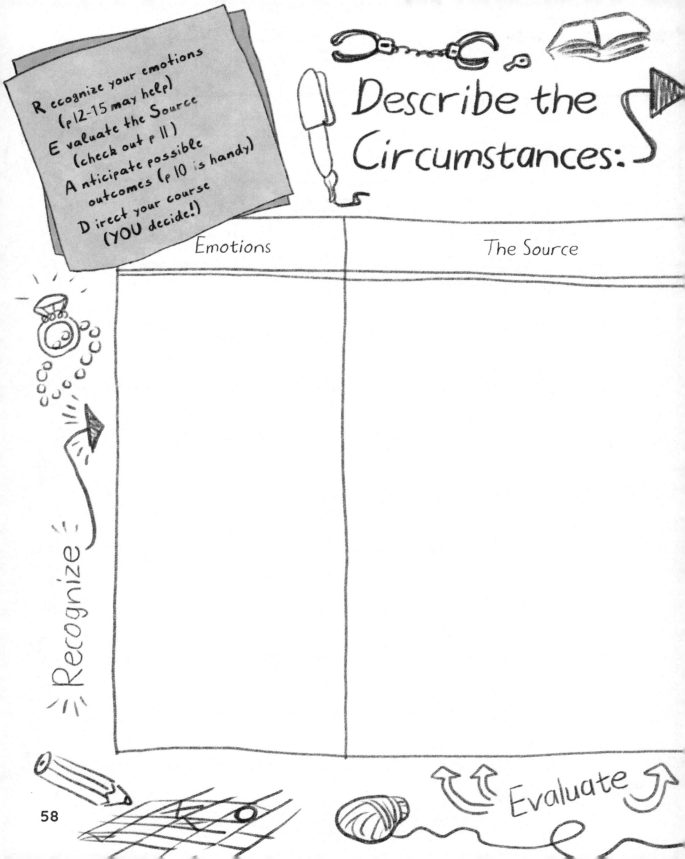

R ecognize your emotions
(p 12-15 may help)
E valuate the Source
(check out p 11)
A nticipate possible
outcomes (p 10 is handy)
D irect your course
(YOU decide!)

Describe the Circumstances:

Emotions	The Source

Recognize

Evaluate

58

_____

_____

_____

Possible Outcome	What will I do?

Anticipate

Direct

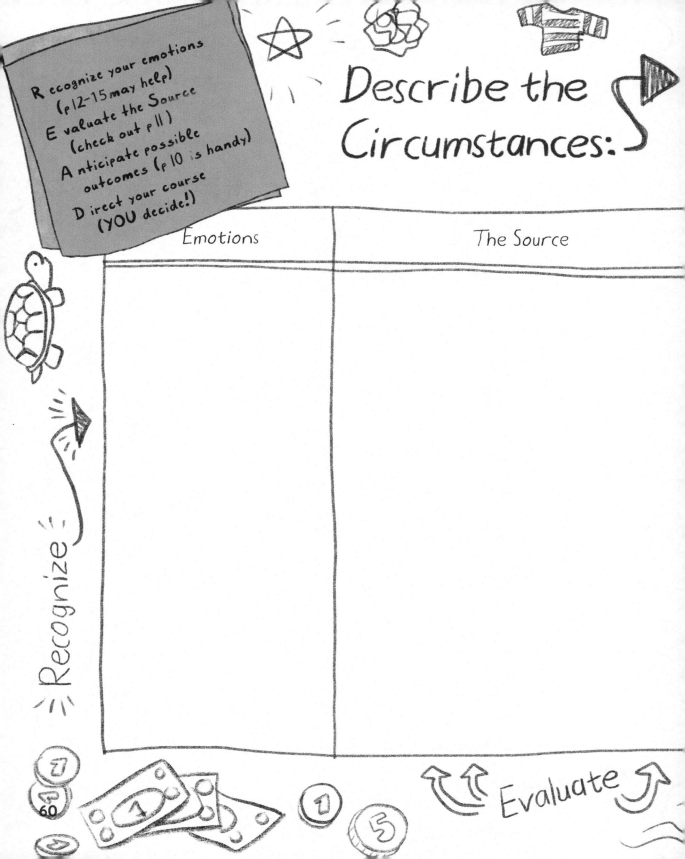

R ecognize your emotions
(p 12-15 may help)
E valuate the Source
(check out p 11)
A nticipate possible
outcomes (p 10 is handy)
D irect your course
(YOU decide!)

Describe the Circumstances:

Emotions	The Source

Recognize

Evaluate

_____

_____

_____

Possible Outcome	What will I do?

Anticipate

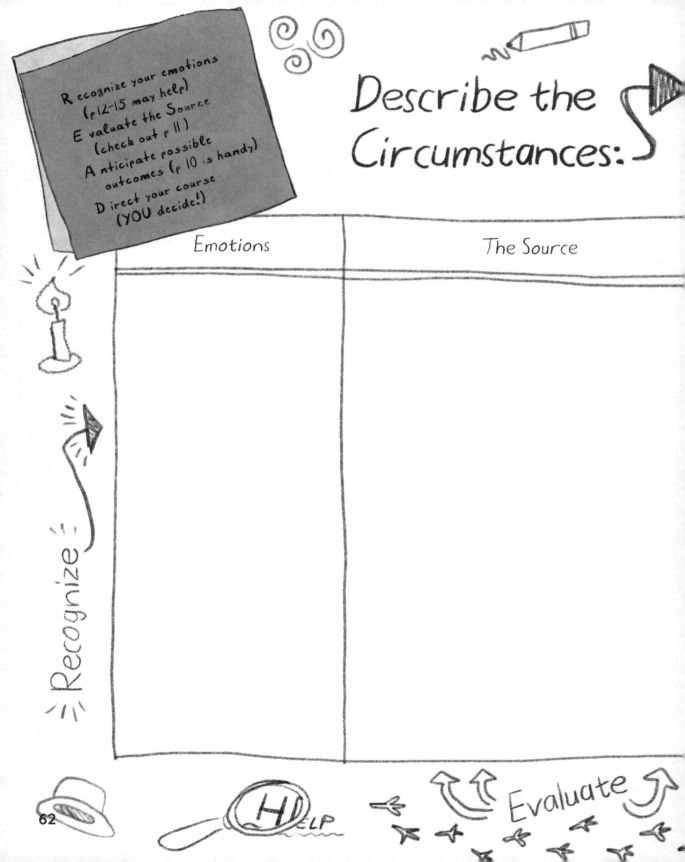

Describe the Circumstances:

R ecognize your emotions
(p 12-15 may help)
E valuate the Source
(check out p 11)
A nticipate possible
outcomes (p 10 is handy)
D irect your course
(YOU decide!)

Emotions	The Source

Recognize

HELP

Evaluate

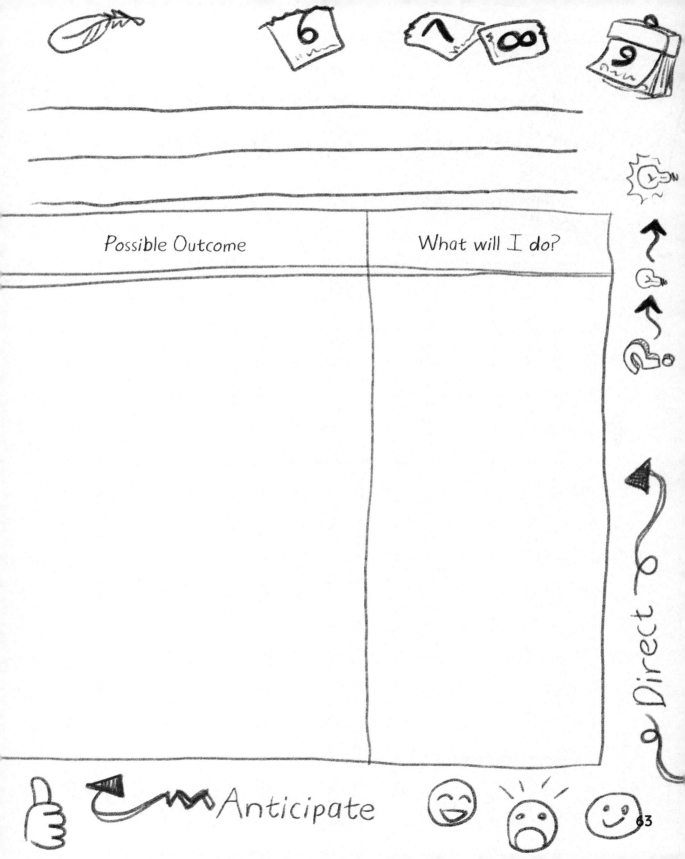

Possible Outcome	What will I do?

Anticipate

Direct

Describe the Circumstances:

Emotions	The Source

Recognize

Evaluate

Possible Outcome	What will I do?

Direct

Anticipate

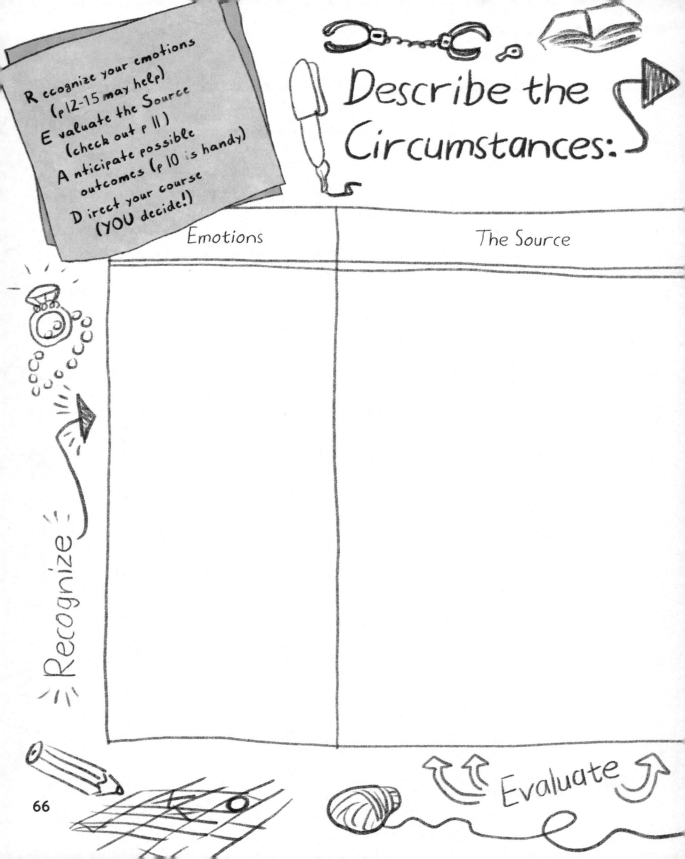

R ecognize your emotions
(p 12-15 may help)
E valuate the Source
(check out p 11)
A nticipate possible
outcomes (p 10 is handy)
D irect your course
(YOU decide!)

Describe the Circumstances:

Emotions	The Source

Recognize

Evaluate

Possible Outcome	What will I do?

Anticipate

Direct

Describe the Circumstances:

Emotions	The Source

Recognize

Evaluate

Possible Outcome	What will I do?

Anticipate

Direct

69

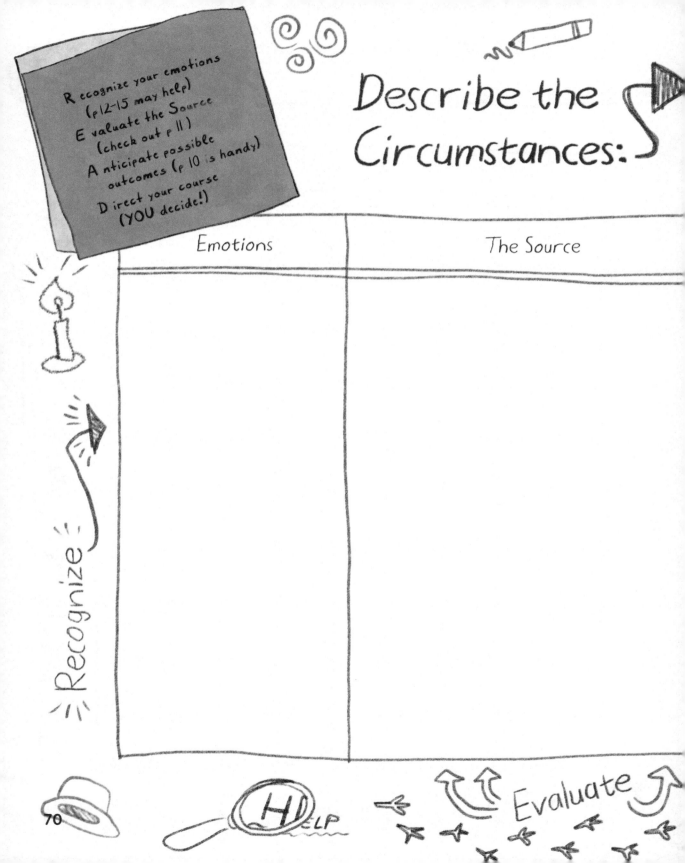

Describe the Circumstances:

R ecognize your emotions
  (p 12-15 may help)
E valuate the Source
  (check out p 11)
A nticipate possible
  outcomes (p 10 is handy)
D irect your course
  (YOU decide!)

Emotions	The Source

Recognize

Evaluate

HELP

Possible Outcome	What will I do?

Anticipate

Direct

Recognize your emotions
(p 12-15 may help)
Evaluate the Source
(check out p 11)
Anticipate possible
outcomes (p 10 is handy)
Direct your course
(YOU decide!)

Describe the Circumstances:

Emotions	The Source

Recognize

Evaluate

Possible Outcome	What will I do?

Anticipate

Direct

73

R ecognize your emotions (p 12-15 may help)
E valuate the Source (check out p 11)
A nticipate possible outcomes (p 10 is handy)
D irect your course (YOU decide!)

Describe the Circumstances:

Emotions	The Source

Recognize

Evaluate

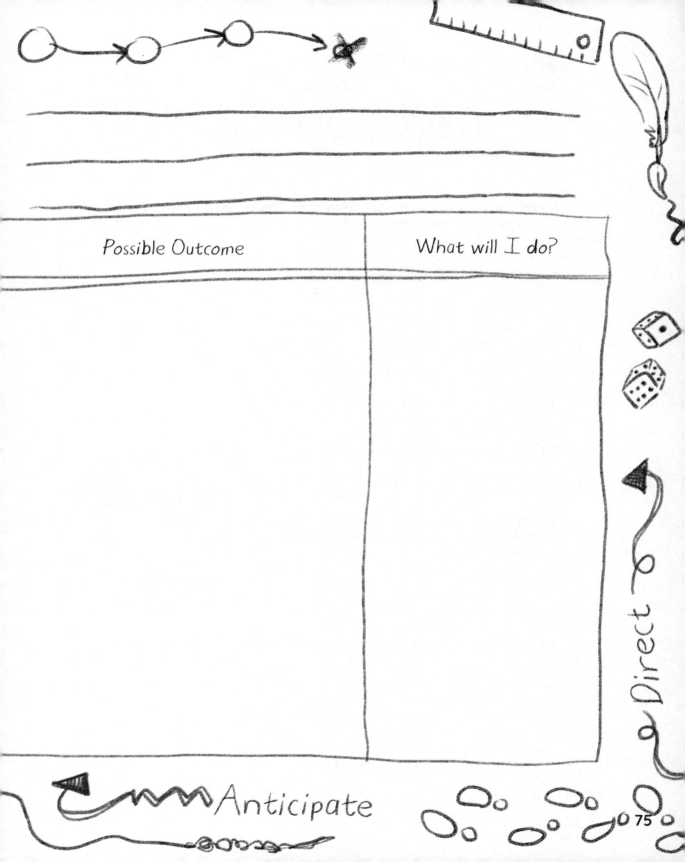

Possible Outcome	What will I do?

Anticipate

Direct

About Relational Wisdom©

1. **Relational wisdom (RW) is the ability to discern emotions, interests and abilities in yourself and others,** to interpret this information in the light of your personal values, and to use these insights to manage your responses and relationships constructively.

2. **RW is a "relational operating system"** (like Windows or Mac OS) that impacts every aspect of our lives, including friendships, marital intimacy, parenting and job performance and advancement.
   - *Relationship trumps expertise* in most areas of life

   - Soft skills *magnify* or *diminish* the value of hard skills
   - Soft skills can account for as much as 80% of success in the marketplace today

3. **Life is all about relationship.**

4. **Relationships can be challenging** because they are often fueled by emotions, both positively and negatively.

5. **RW enables us to deal more effectively with relationships and the emotions that fuel them.**
   - Relationships are three dimensional
     - **Values, Self, Others** (So do continual 360's)
   - Relationships involve two dynamics
     - Awareness: What do I know? (Knowledge)
     - Engagement: What will I do? (Action)

6. **RW involves six relationship-building and leadership skills or disciplines:**
   - Values-Awareness is your ability to honestly identify your true personal values.
   - Values-Engagement is your ability to consistently apply your values to real life.
   - Self-Awareness is your ability to accurately discern your own emotions, thoughts, values, interests and abilities.
   - Self-Engagement is your ability to manage your thoughts, emotions, words and actions.
   - Other-Awareness is your ability to understand and empathize with the experiences, emotions, values and interests of others.
   - Other-Engagement is your ability to love, encourage, serve and resolve differences with others in a mutually beneficial way.

7. Relational wisdom is so simple a child can apply it, yet so complex you can spend the rest of your life developing it. You can start growing today by memorizing and practicing four simple acrostics.

Practice The SOV Plan
- **Self-aware:** How am I feeling and acting?
- **Other-aware:** How are others feeling? How am I affecting them?
- **Values-aware:** What are my values? Am I living them out?

READ Yourself Accurately
- **Recognize** your emotions
- **Evaluate** their source
- **Anticipate** the consequences of following them
- **Direct** them on a constructive course

Follow a Trustworthy GPS
- **Grade** your values (thoughtful reflection)
- **Pursue** worthy values (family, role models)
- **Serve** others (it will make you happier!)

SERVE Every Person You Meet
- **Smile** (Home, office, store, telephone)
- **Explore** and **Empathize** (Show interest and compassion)
- **Reconcile** (Be a peacemaker)
- **Value** (Express appreciation and admiration)
- **Encourage** (Give heart, inspire, put wind under their wings

8. Peacemaking, a special application of RW, is how we draw ourselves and others back inside the RW circle.

The Four G's of Resolving Conflict
- **G**o higher – *live up to your highest values*
- **G**et the log out of your eye – *accept responsibility*
- **G**ently restore – *help others accept responsibility*
- **G**o and be reconciled – *forgive as you want to be forgiven*

Seven A's of Confession
- **A**ddress everyone involved
- **A**void if, but and maybe
- **A**dmit specifically
- **A**cknowledge the hurt
- **A**ccept the consequences
- **A**lter your behavior
- **A**sk for forgiveness

Four Promises of Forgiveness
- I will not dwell on this incident
- I will not bring this incident up and use it against you
- I will not talk with others about this incident
- I will not let this incident hinder our personal relationship

PAUSE Principle of Negotiation
- **P**repare
- **A**ffirm relationships
- **U**nderstand interests
- **S**earch for creative solutions
- **E**valuate options objectively and reasonably

9. Unlike IQ (intelligence quotient) and personality, which do not change noticeably after the teen years, your relational wisdom can improve significantly if you are willing to work at it.
- Download the **RW360 Smartphone App** (www.rw360values.org/app) for hundreds of articles and videos on relational wisdom.
- For insights on the neurology of emotional and relational skills, see Dan Goleman's highly acclaimed books, *Emotional Intelligence* and *Working with Emotional Intelligence*, as well as *Emotional Intelligence 2.0* by Bradberry and Greaves.
- Interactive online training is available at www.rw-academy.org.
- A faith-based version of relational wisdom is available at www.rw360.org.

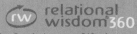

About the Author

Julia Quillen is a homeschool mom of seven. Born and raised in Texas, she now resides in Upper Darby, Pennsylvania. In addition to teaching her kids, Julia is a relationship coach and an Advanced Relational Wisdom® Instructor. She also completed Profiler Training and studied Personality Dynamics at Personality Hacker under the direction of Antonia Dodge and Joel Mark Witt.

Julia started *The Kendry Uto, Detective Series* in response to parents requesting resources to share Relationl Wisdom® skills with their children. Connect with Julia at www.CultivateGrace.org.

About the Illustrator

Maria "Mimi" Hecher is a self-taught illustrator from Austria, currently living in Leipzig, Germany. Since being an entrepreneur on her own and all alone is not much fun, she started an illustrating business with her sister Bibi. You can check out their portfolios at www.hecher-illustration.com.

Mimi works for several self-publishers from all around the world, but she spends most of her time stroking, feeding, watching and playing with her six Maine Coon cats, which is the best hobby ever!

Made in the USA
Columbia, SC
28 August 2022

65669057R00046